THE POWER OF POSITIVE THINKING

THE POWER OF POSITIVE THINKING

Transforming Your Life with Optimism

NOLAN BLACKWOOD

QuillQuest Publishers

CONTENTS

1	Introduction	1
2	Understanding Negative Thinking	5
3	Cultivating a Positive Mindset	9
4	Building Confidence and Self-Esteem	14
5	Harnessing the Power of Visualization	19
6	Overcoming Obstacles and Adversity	23
7	Nurturing Positive Relationships	28
8	Maintaining a Positive Lifestyle	32
9	Spreading Positivity	37
10	Conclusion	41

Copyright © 2024 by Nolan Blackwood

All rights reserved. No part of this book may be reproduced in any manner whatsoever without written permission except in the case of brief quotations embodied in critical articles and reviews.

First Printing, 2024

CHAPTER 1

Introduction

Inside our head, in that small space that no one knows its limits, we can find the most diverse people in the world: there are Arabs, Americans, American Indians, Asians; men, women, adults, and children; there are also famous and unknown; some of them are sick, others are healthy; some of them are rich, others are poor; some of them are happy, many of them are unhappy. This whole group of beings lives in an apartment building with many floors, with a somewhat precarious organization and communication in the building: it is asked that when talking, a person is to make an attempt to know if the listener is able to understand, agree with, or participate in the conversation, the idea being to speed up communication. In this very special building, there is a person who has displayed a huge poster in the main entrance of the building. He has drawn a large half-empty mug, and he asked each of the building's residents to check the water level in the mug and to record whether what was written on the panel was true or not. And as expected, they responded differently: the happy people wrote that it was a half full mug, and the sad people wrote that it was a mug half empty.

Everything starts in the mind, our thoughts. All people experience joy and distress, but how things evolve in reality can be very different. A half full or a half empty glass? Science has discovered that much of what really makes our life good depends on our thoughts. In fact, more than 95% of people feel happier than the average person in the world, so their personal characteristics can have a big influence on personal happiness levels, even more so than personal situations like work, life, health, or social relations. Studies suggest that optimism can teach each one of us to be happier and that this is actually the sentiment that will make us feel happier. This means that it is possible to teach ourselves to think in a different way to be as happy as we want.

1.1. The Importance of Positive Thinking

Martin Seligman establishes that positive thinking and healthy optimism directly contribute to increased skills, while negative thinking leads to complications such as depression, doubt, devaluation, and fear. Positive thoughts and positive people create a healthy environment. On the contrary, pessimism and negative thoughts have negative effects. Negative thoughts also have detrimental effects on our health. Studies have shown a relationship between high levels of stress and heart disease. A study of a group of healthy students at the beginning of their academic careers showed that those with higher levels of specific stress and failure experienced repeated colds, while those with lower levels remained healthy for most of the academic year.

According to the Mayo Clinic, positive thinking helps people live longer lives, experience fewer stress-related illnesses, and have less depression. Positive thinking benefits us mentally and physically, as well as socially and professionally. This kind of thinking creates significant effects that can be important in your life. Society associates optimists with the belief and hope of positive occurrences, increasing the possibility of these occurrences and eliminating feelings of helplessness that pessimists face when dealing with difficulties. How we face reality can directly affect our health. Explanations suggest that positive thinking promotes healthy behaviors in our lives, while negative thinking worsens our state of mind and health. Additionally, people with negative thoughts are often afraid to attempt new things.

1.2. Benefits of Optimism

Become aware of the kind of "self-talk" that is going on in your mind. Whenever you're thinking about and interpreting the events of your day, do you do so in a way that leads you in a positive direction or a negative one? People who think positively do so in much healthier ways. Rather than jumping to conclusions at the slightest reason for avoidance, or interpreting an event as catastrophic or because of something wrong with them that will never change, positive thinkers interpret events of the day (even mistakes or mishaps) as simply little slips that everyone makes. And if you are a healthy person overall, they don't really change you in a very core sense. So, as you consider your self-thought, if you find yourself tending towards the negative path of thinking, STOP, and redirect your thoughts to a more constructive and positive direction.

Optimism can improve your emotional resiliency and physical health. Studies have shown that people who have an optimistic outlook in general are in better health overall and recover more quickly when they fall ill. For instance, positive thinking has been linked to better immune system functioning, longer life spans, and lower rates of depression, cardiovascular disease, and other heart diseases. So if you want to increase your sense of well-being and protect yourself emotionally and physically, you'll want to actively cultivate a healthy and resilient sense of optimism.

1.3. How Positive Thinking Can Transform Your Life

One factor that actually aids physical health is positivity. And if it plays a vital role in one aspect of your life, then it certainly contributes greatly in overall personal development. Think positively and you are preparing your subconscious and conscious minds to achieve greatness, wants, desires, fulfillment... Success. Miracles happen, but not everyone can sit around and wait for one to occur. Positive attitudes are the same as degrees or food – they help prepare you on your journey through life. So, to convert your mind into possessing the great qualities of optimism, ensure that you are surrounding yourself with positive influence. Watch inspiring personal development videos, read motivational and self-help books. One book that I can recommend is "The Power of Positive Thinking" by Norman Vincent Peale. Maintain a conscious effort to only indulge in positive thoughts, and you will convert your mindset over the energy of positivity.

Knowledge allows us to think, believe, and act with more confidence and assurance – because we have actual figures to relate to our businesses and ourselves. Successful minds are positive minds, and mindsets are what separates the winners from the losers. It's basically putting yourself in the right frame of mind. This concept is as simple as it sounds: the more you think positive, the more you'll get positive results. Your mind plays a powerful role in achieving better health, and many medical professionals say that good mental health can help treat, and effectively treat, many bodily ailments.

CHAPTER 2

Understanding Negative Thinking

The problem for most people, however, is life with its challenges and difficulties takes its toll. Good news generally elicits little more than a weary smile from most people. "It's just the way life is," one former patient, a 60-year-old woman, said to me. "I can't expect anything more." No complaints, no tearful rants about the weather or other annoyances, only weighty, resolute acceptance. For many, negative thoughts have become so dominant that they've ceased seeing them as limited, provisional responses to particular situations. Rather, they have accepted them as absolute truth, perceiving contrary opinions as so way off base that they either don't notice or view them as naive and obnoxious. Why does this happen? It happens because negative thinking is dangerous. Not only does it feel comfortable, calming, ready to lovingly embrace doubts, anxieties, and fears, but it is also the manner in which we hide from and cope with the sudden, ludicrous demands life places on us. Not knowing what else to do, many of us respond to the vagaries of life by developing negative attitudes and behaviors, thereby acquiring an all-purpose safety valve.

When confronted with a patient's negative thinking, caregivers may grow impatient. After all, telling someone to see the glass as half full and not half empty just doesn't work. And yet, evidence clearly demonstrates that optimism is beneficial to your health and your life. A study found that women with low self-esteem had a risk of 175 percent over the course of eight years of developing heart disease compared to those with high self-esteem. Optimists are in a better mood, physically healthier, and often emotionally more balanced. They have better chances of living to a ripe old age, of surviving cancer, and achieving success in their professional and private lives. Is it any wonder, then, that optimists are so liked and sought after?

2.1. Recognizing Negative Thought Patterns

When learning to recognize negative thought patterns, it is helpful to seek the assistance of objective and caring people who can provide feedback. If we ask them to help us identify and stop our own negative comments that they may observe, they often can. Engaging in healthy arguments about the quality of our thinking is a good way to replace negative comments with more constructive ones. One of the most important steps in learning how to diminish our negative thoughts and feelings is to consciously drop the belief that our negativity serves a useful purpose. A number of positive thought patterns, complete with appropriate challenges to self-defeating negative thoughts and beliefs, have been developed and popularized. Many of these beliefs reflect habits of thinking that can be adapted to suit each individual.

The first step toward harnessing the power of positive thinking is recognizing our own negative thought patterns. To do so requires self-awareness. By learning to recognize our own unique habitually negative thought patterns, we can begin to replace them with positive thoughts. We can learn cognitive tools that help us to stop or modify negative thought patterns and replace them with constructive, positive ones. It is important to know and avoid common mistakes that can actually increase negativity.

2.2. The Impact of Negative Thinking on Mental Health

The direct relations are less consistent but it is possible to say that negative automatic thoughts are associated with greater daily mood variability and anxiety. Some of the results also suggest that thought patterns function as mediators in the sense that how anxious a person feels depends somewhat on the thoughts that the person has. Thus, it is very likely that negative automatic thoughts lead to daily mood variability via the experience of fear and anxiousness. These assumptions have been made almost while investigating how these thought patterns result in generalized anxiety and in the PAD model, an approach that has gained a good amount of supportive findings since its inception.

I'd say that the cognitive trap that most of us are most susceptible to is overgeneralizing and thinking that smaller and less frequent events may be representative of your reality. This is when you start overthinking and come to a conclusion that something manageable and small might cause a catastrophic outcome. When we think of highlights, we often first think of studies that suggest that people are anxious because they overestimate the probability of negative events. However, there is an equal amount of research that shows that people base their feelings of anxiousness on how awful the possible negative outcome could be if it did actually happen. Unfortunately, the studies also suggest that people with low self-esteem might be especially likely to think of very bad outcomes and therefore, experience a great deal of distress when thinking about far from certain and fairly small risks.

2.3. Overcoming Negative Thinking

Be peaceful in your faith, and your fears will help you guard against all forms of vice that you will encounter on your journey. If you allow it, your own faith will help you overcome life's daily struggles. Confiding in the spiritual strength of Christ will help you disentangle these strands that subjugate all of us in weakness. All too often, the bad habits that we self-justify unleash worldwide. Gain more confidence by constantly imitating the life of Christ in every detail of your life. With daily practice that at first produces amazing results of self-discipline, perseverance, and general diligence, it will not be long before God grants your reasonable request. You will then once again regard long-term effort as a very pleasant pastime.

Overcoming negative thinking takes a thoughtful approach. If you indulge in some negative thinking, over time your perception of reality becomes the lens through which you regard the world around you. If you surround yourself with negative people, you will become deeply affected by their view of life and its circumstances. However, if you surround yourself with positive individuals, you will see life in a whole new light. People tend to make a fuss about seemingly unimportant matters or bad decisions; that is, if it has negative consequences affecting their life, they refuse to be fooled any longer by anyone or anything. They are in no mood to be industrious, working industriously to indulge every human frailty. When one's circumstances are at a record low in life, people may exhibit these traits listed above. Instead, foster an enthusiasm to lead an outstandingly regulated life that to many would seem to be entrusted with an impossible power through the Name of Christ.

CHAPTER 3

Cultivating a Positive Mindset

Negative thinking starts early in one's life. At school and at home, we often heard messages that remained deeply entrenched in our psyche. These negative messages should be replaced with positive ones. You must treat yourself as you would treat a good friend. If you treat yourself kindly and supportively, you will be better able to deal with whatever life throws at you, no matter the source. You must see the exceptional person you are. Seeking the support of others is unnecessary. You are not superfluous. You have a mission to carry out in this world. By helping others, you affirm your value and significance. What you give comes back to you. Perhaps the person you helped will help you in turn.

To cultivate a positive mindset, we must turn our self-talk, the ongoing conversation in our head, from negative to positive. Many people allow their self-talk to be overly negative or to spin out of control when problems are coming at them, they are surrounded by negative people, or they are in the habit of seeing the glass as half-empty. According to Dr. Robert Schuller, minister, motivational speaker, and author of many best-selling books, there are different steps to take in cultivating a positive mindset. The first one is to stop speaking negatively about yourself. If we turn to the Golden Rule, "Do unto others as you would have them do unto you," we can see that it certainly applies to the way we treat others. However, it also applies to ourselves. If we would not tolerate others speaking to us the way we speak to ourselves, then why do we treat ourselves the way we do? It is a mystery for many people.

3.1. Developing Self-Awareness

Fortunately, the development of self-awareness does not stop despite the lack of attention in traditional education. As you grow, you may become keenly aware of those elements in your repertoire of thinking and speech that you recognize as your own. As a result, you eventually learn to separate that over which you have some control from that which controls you. Your education often includes the realization that the person you believe yourself to be encompasses both a conscious and an unconscious mind, and that much of your behavior springs from an automatic, if not instinctive, response from the unconscious. Since your education often comes at a high price, you may realize that these concealed elements within yourself lead to words and deeds for which you must be responsible even if they are unknown to you.

From our earliest years, parents and other adults constantly prod us to behave. As a child, you have little choice but to comply; otherwise, you would face unpleasant consequences such as punishment or the loss of parental approval. Over time, you utter and behave in response to increasingly complex stimuli. With encouragement and sometimes coercion, you add languages, customs, and values to your repertoire of activities. Often driven by the demands of others, you may reach adulthood feeling that your speech and behavior arise from outside you. You may find it hard, even impossible, to distinguish between speech and behavior derived from your own thinking and other people's expectations or conventional speech patterns.

3.2. Practicing Gratitude

So how does one practice gratitude? I usually advise students, particularly those who are disillusioned by the large class sizes at the workshop, or those who experience a major life event such as a job strain up or relationship breakdown, to write a gratitude journal and walk away from negative comparisons towards grounded connection. Besides this, one can perform acts of kindness in service of increasing the experiences of gratitude. The act of going through emotional upheavals and then noting gratitude is not only a testimony of living in gratitude but it is also a strong indicator of resilience. Envisaging future goals and moves at work may make an office ambiance seem vibrant and appealing, but only when a substantial part of your employees, teams, and even other stakeholders are experiencing gratitude will you be on the first rung in developing an optimistic environment.

So how can we cultivate a feeling of gratitude amid the rush of life? There are many simple things one can do to build up feelings of gratitude in everyday situations. These include consolidating your goals, creating to-do lists, practicing intentional gratification, and spending less time comparing yourself with others. Groundbreaking studies on intentional activities to increase happiness indicate that people doing these activities do get happier. But what seems to be more impactful is the strategy of practicing gratitude. The practice of living in gratitude involves feeling whole and thankful for what one already possesses mentally instead of focusing and visualizing new goals with the hope to acquire them.

3.3. Surrounding Yourself with Positive Influences

Cultivating a circle of positive people is a way to ensure that you don't fall into a destructive pattern. The friends and family you keep close are often a reflection of your own thought patterns and mindset. Having people around you who have embraced a healthy, positive outlook will make it much easier to stay on the right track. When you see friends who face challenges and setbacks with a positive outlook and achieve their goals, you know you can do it, too, and it's always easier to keep that idea in your head when someone close to you has reinforced it.

It's often said that you are the company you keep. There's just something about positive individuals that can't help but energize and uplift the room. Make it a point to surround yourself with others who value positive thinking and let their outlook enrich your life. A good, strong circle of friends who give off this energy is invaluable. They're so much more than just people to spend time with; they're your support network and your sounding board. They can remind you that you have setbacks and that things don't always work out the way you want them to, but you can learn from those setbacks and apply those lessons to new goals and tasks. They can point out what you're doing right and what you're doing wrong.

3.4. Embracing Change and Resilience

The concept of change is very broad and complex, being understood by some people as devastating, painful, and hurtful; also being understood as the possibility of advancement, development, innovation, update, and new experiences. Change for good, when a person perceives positivity in something new and confronts challenges, grows, and develops. Negative change, however, is when something new is viewed with pessimism, denoting fear of exiting the comfort zone to confront adversities. However, sometimes such negative change is inevitable, making people develop the capacity to overcome sources of immeasurable pain beyond human limits. A grave crime against human dignity, it left dozens of survivors with no hope of attaining normalcy, happiness, and peace of mind. Analyzing the history and sociocultural representations and bringing alongside Viktor Frankl and his concepts, it is possible to understand the development of resilience, which undoubtedly has everything to do with the ability of individuals to seek goals and pursue the meaning of life, that is, to believe in the future and move toward it with determination, as well as seek tranquility and spiritual freedom so that joy, optimism, and love remain alive.

Through the power of positive thinking, people are able to reduce their stress levels and better cope with challenges and change in their lives. Changing technologies and social support help develop resilience in individuals and improve human relationships. Resilience is an ability or a skill that can be learned, promoting the individual's self-esteem and the harmony of their surroundings. By reinforcing the changes a person encounters, they manage to reduce the negative impacts brought by them. Through resilience, the individual manages to adapt to different situations, constantly changing their behavior to overcome the challenges faced. The ability to overcome adversities is an indispensable characteristic for those who want to remain strong and optimistic in the face of unexpected and undesirable situations because it is up to the individual to find their strength in their own weaknesses.

CHAPTER 4

Building Confidence and Self-Esteem

Self-esteem is an individual's total emotional assessment of human worth in relation to others (e.g., how much praise and criticism one receives, how accepted one is). This judges how someone values himself or herself when receiving judgment from others. While the term "verbal abuse" helps identify harsh comments a child may receive during their formative years, by parents, teachers or adult peers, for example, "self-esteem abuse" refers to the means people abuse themselves without even recognizing that they do it. Dr. Abramson said that a hallmark of major depression is pervasive low self-esteem. There are all sorts of different dynamics that occur in relationships between self-esteem and other domains. He also thinks that there is a certain inertia; once someone's self-esteem gets to a certain level, gravity takes over. That is, there is a gravitational pull of self-esteem in one domain dragging down the others. In a way, good things just don't happen for people who see themselves as losers.

Life presents many twists and turns, but the essence of all anyone can allow themselves to become spirals from individual differentiation. Knowing that you have something distinct to offer to the world—or to others around you—will surely boost your self-confidence. Conversely, it's essential to remember that one of the most unpleasant human emotions is vanity. Being confident doesn't mean that you should fasten onto arrogance or superiority. That usually leads to deep-rooted lack of confidence and can cause personal complexities with labor and personal relationships. In general, it will simply make you distasteful to be around. Forcing yourself into the unpleasant limelight of conduct means taking your mind off what's essential in life. The extreme passion for oneself also takes away the pith of living.

4.1. Challenging Limiting Beliefs

It must be recognized that each of us has inherent strengths and weaknesses. Uncovering our own strengths at times can be testing, especially if our abilities are at the subconscious level. Herein, keeping a journal is recommended. This will allow an avenue for revelations to make their way into our everyday. Three limiting beliefs, in the present writer's opinion, follow. These may not necessarily be adopted as one's own limiting beliefs, although likely to be more general than not. The first limiting belief is that words must have some measurable quality for them to be considered significant. This is a limiting belief by virtue of supplying a poor measuring tool. There are folk stories as well as ancient wisdom that guide conduct and morality very effectively without needing to be a factual account of events. A comforting realization presents itself here through Lord Tennyson's words: "Truth embodied in a tale shall enter in at lowly doors." (It's not what you know, but who you know seems to have roots stretching beyond our present knowledge!)

Beliefs can limit us significantly. They can limit our growth and capacity to see opportunities and abundant possibilities that are in our midst. It's important to be aware of any limiting beliefs we have and examine the context in which they have existed and whether it is still relevant. The challenging of limiting beliefs can be both external, such as through reading and learning, or internal by digging deep and examining ourselves. The objective is likely to be more successful if it is carried out by both mediums. Also of note is the importance of the company we keep, for we tend to behave as the people we spend the most time with. This is because our beliefs create our reality and then our reality reinforces our belief. As George Samuel Clements said, "If I say it long enough, I'm going to believe it." This is why it's important to deliberately choose the company we keep.

4.2. Setting Realistic Goals

When we meet challenges with effort, anxiety disappears and although the task continues to be difficult, we will no longer perceive its demands as stress. We will develop hope, which allows us to "keep our chins up" with optimism, capable of renewing itself daily. And we will direct our actions within the time structure indicated, creating a greater probability of success. We must bear in mind that our life on a timetable does not stop and will always be indifferent to our personal circumstances. In fact, this structure should be considered as a source of peace because we will feel that we are moving forward in life.

We will benefit from firm and realistic objectives, defined over time, according to a plan, considering the resources we have available. Therefore, the phrase "I take what comes" – valid as a philosophy of life – fails to fulfill the function of positioning us before the present moment and what happens to us. This is what Dr. Jose Maria Vicedo has called "The concept of encountering good fortune," and which should be a long-term goal in addition to those goals achieved that we are also happy about. When stressful situations arrive, blocking us at a given instant and making it impossible to move forward a little more on the road to happiness, it is important to always keep this encounter in mind. Close-to-reality and long-term goals have many advantages for our lives. For example, failures lose importance. If we have a job interview two or three days after we've been fired, we'll see it differently.

There has been a trend in recent years in which entrepreneurs and business owners have taken to following the latest procedures for setting goals at both a personal and a professional level. To this end, specialists have developed a system that takes into account not only how the mind works, but also organizational objectives. One of these techniques is known as a SWOT (strengths, weaknesses, opportunities, and threats) analysis. With a SWOT analysis, we evaluate what advantages and strengths we have in order to take advantage of opportunities and how to eliminate or soften our weaknesses in the face of threats.

4.3. Celebrating Personal Achievements

It really is the small things that help to fortify my confidence in personal abilities. Any morning I spend writing for myself, having a scheduled park adventure with my grandmothers in the afternoon, an evening night held for me to converse with my little brother, or a bedtime learning of incredible war experiences. I want to remind myself of these days when I feel incredibly grateful, adaptive, energized, or moments when I was able to guide and educate those around me in some form. I want to remind myself of them only for them to represent that perseverance, dedication, and appreciation of my surrounding world will help me overcome or even come to value all my challenges. Success in my eyes is to overcome these challenges or even a closing of these frustrations, and I hope the following days and events will be leading down a more positive road, to create life as the beautiful journey in which it really is. I note in my diary all of these glorious happenings in my life.

You cannot move forward with a positivity-filled mindset if you are dragged down with an air of frustration and failure. If you experience small successes, celebrate them. This is so crucial to keep the positive energy in your life so that you can continue to move through it – and take time to reflect on or celebrate the success. You also can't give yourself any slack by not celebrating these moments! I tend to be shy when I receive praise from others and just brush it off, but really I should be rejoicing over my little triumphs and then giving thanks to every person that helped me achieve them. Hopefully, this will motivate me to continue making ethical decisions and create positive impacts on the world. Sometimes I may need to pat myself on the back and share a proud moment with those close to me, and that's crucial. A moment is a success and "a realization that I may seize and feast upon".

CHAPTER 5

Harnessing the Power of Visualization

Researchers have found that although you can't change your genes, you can change how they are expressed. Genes are - obviously - the instructions for making things like protein, which is necessary for biological life. Also obviously, your genetic code doesn't change from birth. But what happens - and is quite extraordinary in its implications for your health and longevity - is that the expression of these genes change, as do the levels of the protein that is made from the gene. Even small changes in gene expression can have profound effects. Take a look at the image to the left (For a larger view, see p. 28), which shows two mice who are exactly the same age but with different levels of a particular protein - pink areas show the protein is expressed and not suppressed. As you will see, the mouse on the right has profoundly less suppressed protein 1:60 versus 1:220.

Many experts recommend the power of visualization as a means for improving your life. In part, the recommendation involves your commitment to whatever it is you are trying to attain. By visualizing your success, you become mentally and emotionally attached to the goal, so you'll be more committed to achieving it. This doesn't mean such goals are easier to reach. It simply means that you are much more likely to persist and to put in the hard work necessary to achieve the goal. There is also evidence to suggest that widespread physical and molecular changes in the body occur when using visualization as a means to depict success - in particular changing brain activity patterns.

5.1. Creating a Vision Board

Not every woman is going to have the same content on their board, and that is what makes them absolutely beautiful! We are all unique and amazing. One thing you can add to keep yourself on track is your top three goals for 2015. Visualization is one of the most powerful exercises in the world! What we believe in, something we can achieve =) Once the board is all finished and beautiful, I usually hang the vision board right above my computer for easy motivation I can see from my desk every day.

To start, when the board is finished, I will begin adding all of the accomplishments I have listed up into the corner of the board. I love the idea of not being able to cover them all up with my hand as they build up year after year. This is also the perfect place to add your word of the year. It is also a very motivational tool, to keep a list on the side of your board of all the things you would like to have on your board in the future. This is great to do at the beginning of your board to keep yourself motivated along the way. In the past, I also did my favorite Bible verse of the year and business card to represent where I was working. This helped me visualize what I want out of my business.

5.2. Visualizing Success

Your brain takes your images literally, as does your body photography. If you close your eyes and try to produce a vivid mental image of, say, a cat, you will see it's so realistic—like the real thing, only in your mind. This goes for everything in life—you can create and access stored resources by simply living what you want through intense visualization. Truthfully, you can change the way your body functions and feels with visualization alone. For example, J. Kip Matthews, a sports psychology consultant, revealed in an email exchange that "brain scans performed on individuals who just imagined themselves lifting weights showed a neural pattern similar to those who actually did the physical lifting." You can create these experiences by yourself, where you can change your life. Relax, breathe, and put yourself in a hypnotic trance by visualizing what you desire. The paradox of this phenomenon is this: If you don't believe it works, then that's exactly what will happen and your brain will focus on doubt, triggering negativity.

Visualization is a powerful way to manifest the desires of our hearts. Visualizing daily brings added clarity to our positive thinking, helping us access inner resources we wouldn't have known we had. The process can lead to a tidal wave of motivation, transforming our most passionate dreams into viable reality. If you study the most successful athletes in the world, visual imagery is a tried-and-true method for their success. Olympic athletes report using visualization techniques over 90 percent of the time. When Émile Coué said "Day by day, in every way, I am getting better and better," he meant that he visualized his successes, internalizing what he wanted in a very intentional way. Without doubt, the immense belief and visualization methods employed by Anthony Robbins and dozens of other celebrities are grounds for more optimism. Equally important, if you haven't had success at this stage, pretending you are the person you'd like to become makes a big difference.

5.3. Using Affirmations to Reinforce Positive Thinking

A great way to practice affirmation is to use them when you wake up or go to bed. Recurrent reminders really help solidify the neural pathways you're trying to achieve. And yes, practice is key. For example, how many times do you have to repeat this information before you memorize it? Your goal is to make this type of memorization connect as closely as possible to making positive affirmations: the same need to practice to retain.

When we set goals and repeat them frequently, we begin to accept them as true and viable. Consciousness is a web of simple interactions creating complex channels of activity across the folds of the human brain; repeating these channels creates a deeper and grooved system of connections that become much more implicit. In simpler terms, practicing tasks and affirmations can make achieving goals easier. It takes about 21 days of practice to create a lasting connection in the neural pathways for an activity or affirmation. It may take some time to alter your thought patterns, but if you use reminders and practice, it can enhance your mental health.

Here are some examples of good affirmative thoughts to consider: "I am healthy, happy and radiant", "Positive energy flows through me like water through a stream", "Everything I experience and everything I feel is a beautiful lesson that beholds a silver lining", "I embrace the world's diversity and see it as a teacher", "I enjoy a life full of continuous transformation, even when faced with stagnation", "I am successful, both in personal and shared ventures" and "I am surrounded with an abundance of love and mental stimulation".

CHAPTER 6

Overcoming Obstacles and Adversity

I know that opening yourself to such a powerful change may seem frightening. You may feel like you are taking a leap of faith. But in the process of understanding and implementing optimism - self-reflection is of the utmost importance. Try to spend ten minutes every single day alone and reflect on the great things you have experienced. And don't be afraid to display that dialogue to yourself. It's not a sign of madness - merely your mind's attempts to unravel problems and reflections to the outside world. Next up, smile more! Even when the problem you face is enormous. Smiling doesn't provide an immediate solution to all of your problems. However, it can open the window to your heart, allowing optimism and happiness to enter it. A positive mind is a powerful friend - it is capable of anything and everything! Always remember that positive thoughts generate a positive heart, which has the potential to create positive behavior - this chain reaction can serve as a tool that will help us create an optimism revolution within us. Remember that optimism is much more than shallow, everyday joy. The power of positive thinking will bring success, joy, as well as a sense of happiness and fulfillment that cannot be taken away from you, despite life's trials and tribulations. An optimistic mind allows us to perceive difficult situations as challenges that can be overcome, whereas a pessimist will be instantly conquered by the mere thought of adversity.

Before you start taking practical steps to transform your attitude and emotions, it may be difficult for you to believe that merely trying to replace negative thoughts with positive ones can create significant changes in your life. And yet, with time and effort, the impossible can and will become possible! What's more, this optimism and belief in yourself will be contagious. As you begin to display positive behavior, those around you will also start subconsciously adopting your positive attitude. It is a powerful and beautiful process that is relatively simple to initiate yet can be extremely effective and transformational when used properly. Remember that a small act of kindness can change the world. Always aim at better, to awaken the feeling of optimism and hope in your colleagues, employees, friends, and family. You will make their lives better!

We live in a society full of adversity and uncertainty. Every single day - from the moment you set foot in public transport or start watching the morning news until you're bombarded with emails before going to sleep - you are exposed to pessimistic attitudes only. Bad news, personal problems, people criticizing and speaking negatively about others, and a lot of other negative stimuli that surround us are extremely toxic and can infect your mind and soul. This is why it is of the utmost importance that you learn and practice the art of optimism and active smile.

6.1. Developing a Growth Mindset

There was a time, until last year, when I did not recognize the power of my potential, let alone the growth potential. I had the lowest form of self-esteem about myself, and those were tough days.

But gradually, when I started working on what I should do and by taking small steps, I began to recognize the greatness within me. I began to acknowledge my high self-worth, which helped me to progress by investing in high potential opportunities. As I reflected upon the good things that were happening, I realized that I had been practicing a growth mindset all along, and it was helping me to progress pragmatically. It was no different than the excitement of a child who solely parents himself in the absence of his parent.

Our mind works in excellent ways, one of them being the psychology of mindset coined by Prof. Carol Dweck. She has been working on it for a long time, understanding the workings of a growth mindset and a fixed mindset. The latest book by her talks about mindset, and she has discussed some experiments that help to create a growth mindset in the readers. But if we delve deeper into the subject, we would understand that it is not just a mere mindset that can help one grow. What is really required is the practice of a growth mindset, and that truly transforms one's life. Let me try to explain this with my life experience.

6.2. Finding Opportunity in Challenges

The great philosopher, Confucius, rightly affirms, "The superior man is modest in his speech, but surpasses in his actions." If we wish to transform our life with optimism, then we should start with positivity in speech and exceed in our actions. When we live with an optimistic, positive mind, we are transformed, and we help others to be so. Positive thinking in oneself, positive appreciation of others, and an optimistic approach to situations, particularly in adverse situations, emanate from kindness and love. Positive thinking brings joy and peace and manifests as success and happiness. A bad person is one who gradually influences others to hate life, whereas a good person is one who inspires others to love life. As Mr. Michael Edmondson aptly remarks: "Expect the best and the best that is what you will receive." It brings inner peace, helps to attract true thoughts, resolves conflicts, and makes us look inward. Therefore, let us bow to positive thankfulness and transform our life with optimism and live for the well-being of all.

An NC State lecturer recently sparked my interest with an interesting lecture. Michael Edmondson from Poole College of Management talked about the power of positive thinking and transforming life with optimism. He gave the lecture on the occasion of a leadership and success conference day organized by eMentorConnect. The lecture was informative, fun, and intriguing. Mr. Edmondson's experiences, his stories, and research data in psychology gave us a new discernment. What struck me most was Mr. Edmondson's emphasis on finding opportunity in challenges. He highlighted that optimistic and positive thinking makes people see the opportunity in every challenge, whereas a pessimistic attitude makes people see the challenge in every opportunity.

6.3. Building Resilience in the Face of Adversity

2. Create habits, manage negative thinking, and support individuals' physical and mental health. We are experiencing incredibly high levels of stress and anxiety. This precipitates sadness, feelings of anger, and frustration. To change the focus of the negative thoughts, try to interrupt the torrent of that can make everything negative, making an effort to redirect the thinking towards positive things, confirm encouraging memories, or consider the quality of themselves. Doing well. Developing or reinforcing a habit of praising oneself and replacing negative thoughts with positive ones, such as gratitude, can help in mental and physical health. Regular exercise, a diet based on the consumption of fruits, vegetables, and protein, and maintaining adequate sleep can also help maintain a good mood. Encourage you to do the same and make a commitment to end unhealthy behavior, such as alcohol and drug use.

1. Make social connections. Connect with family members, partners, colleagues, and friends (you have someone to help you). Relationships with other people are the most important sources of comfort and support. They are a wonderful way to help you understand that you are not alone. Just having someone who listens to you during exposure to highly stressful events can be healing. A mutual exchange of help and support is also important. Whether social support comes from family, friends, or a companion, it is important to take time to make those connections. Phone calls, video chats, or social media networks can help you stay connected with others.
1. Some people have the power to face adversity and bounce back with a new life interest, or they are even better after the problem than they were before. One important reason these particular individuals are able to deal with adversity so effectively is that they are more resilient. True resilience comes from deep within individuals, and no matter how many efforts are made, somehow the person will be better as a result of the problem. In my professional work as a therapist, clients often ask to be assisted in this process of developing resilience in the face of adversities. Here are some suggestions to build resilience.

CHAPTER 7

Nurturing Positive Relationships

Altruism, kindness, and empathy can offset some of the negative effects of combativeness, hostility, or competition, and may generate positive emotions and relationships. Friendliness, for example, helps to create close and supportive friendships, which can be uplifting. Positive relations with family members can also help to shape your character in positive ways. Congenial exchanges bolster positive sentiments and yield assorted rewards. Furthermore, engaging in pro-social conduct can contribute to your own emotional well-being by promoting positive emotions, acknowledging and validating yourself as a kind and helpful person, and upholding a positive identity.

Your responses to others can foster positive feelings or provoke hostility. In interpersonal relations, the Golden Rule dictates sound conduct: Do unto others as you would have them do to you. Showing patience, tact, sensitivity, courtesy, friendliness, and concern for other people can boost their self-esteem and result in positive interaction. Such exchanges can strengthen personal relationships by producing cheerful, loving, forgiving, empathetic, and supportive behaviors. By increasing harmonious interaction, endorsement of the Golden Rule fosters a climate for improving psychological well-being. Positive interplay can also help to protect you from harmful events or distress caused by others. You can promote safe, healthy, and ample interaction throughout your life. At the same time, emphasizing the Golden Rule will discourage negative behavior, such as prejudice, condescension, disrespect, intolerance, suspicion, and spite.

7.1. Communicating Effectively

Meanwhile, according to the principles we are discussing, this means (in the other individual's relationship to the creative effort of the first) internal cooperation and participation but no direct dominance or control. With all factors cooperative, with physical, emotional and mental elements harmoniously balanced, each individual involved in the creative problems employs his skills and knowledge and, perhaps most importantly, skills and knowledge yet to be developed, in providing a building process for cooperation that, much like water running over stones on the beach, seeks every door, every conceivable opening, and provides usable and tested solutions, without emotional failure.

One of the reasons for the discord that may come when individuals put into practice these principles of cooperative creativity is a lack of communication and goal sharing. Many people have been strongly influenced, emotionally and intellectually, by the competitive system, and it is hard for anybody to completely free themselves from the patterns of the past. There must be freedom to discuss one's most deeply held ideas and theories with another, and this freedom must be held inviolate and treated with respect and understanding if real cooperation is to take place. The true creative individual, the true poet of life, may hear what another has to say and also may understand what another does not say (due to pressures, fears, or hesitations) and understand the implications or obstacles that lay in the way.

7.2. Practicing Empathy and Understanding

You could be surprised at the overflow of internal restructuring in your motivation, interpersonal bonds, and cognitive operations with a relatively simple reorganizing of actions and desires. By offering your concerns and understanding, you would be empowering your social network with shield designs having a reassuring, comparable organismal backbone, strengthened against pathogenic challenges and somber emotions. Together we could bask in brighter, more restorative lives which bear witness to the maturing, responsible morphologies of strength and peace. We can watch awe colorful persona expressions, which symbolize the sources of our affections and stunning differences. With your hands, your mind, and your heart, you can influence others' lives for the better. Together we can move towards assurance of the realization of the evolved, complete human existence that we most richly deserve.

There is almost certainly someone in your life, or perhaps there are several people, who you could give a little more of yourself. If so, you likely have what it takes to serve as a very effective "still face" partner, offering your steadfast attention and understanding through times of strain or tribulation. You can express explicitly that you will be there for someone in need and show sympathy, according to loaded predictions about physical and psychological improvements now thought to be initiated at increasing cellular levels in a giving individual. At the same time, the widespread availability of extrinsic and intrinsic rewards would likely aid associations of participating in empathic endeavors as those with positive emotions and improved prospects concomitantly arrive. Participating in help for another, who is undergoing difficulties, or illness warmly underscores and potentially strengthens social support bonds which otherwise might gradually erode due to now lessened appreciation of psychological, physical, and resourceful value or availability of the relationship.

7.3. Surrounding Yourself with Supportive People

The practice of positive thinking can greatly affect our physical well-being. This is one of the most important connections widely acknowledged by both medical professionals and spiritual healers. In recent years, a number of scientific studies have shown that physical health reaps considerable benefit from positive mental attitudes, including an increased response to immunization. This leap in faith to the broader scientific community is creating expanding medical research in the country concerning the potential consequences of negative and positive thinking on health status by emphasizing the relationships between thoughts and emotions from a multidisciplinary perspective. New technologies are allowing us to investigate interactions and feedbacks between body, mind, and feelings that would not have been imagined some years ago. Deep changes in molecular and cellular biology are preparing the ground for these advances by rescuing more mechanistic studies toward an integration with cognitive, social, and personal factors. Achieving a complete understanding of these relationships is a challenging but fascinating scientific task.

In "The Power of Negative Thinking," we looked at some of the devastating consequences of pessimistic thinking: depression, anxiety, shyness, and poor health. It is natural to wonder if negative thinking can have such profound effects, can positive thinking bring us to a happier existence? Just imagine how different your life could be if you could learn to relate, react, and interpret events and ideas in a fundamentally better way. Not only are there immense and external benefits to positive thinking, but it can also bring about a tremendous shift in our physical health. Positive thinking also contributes to our physical well-being.

CHAPTER 8

Maintaining a Positive Lifestyle

Positive interaction with others is an essential aspect of a positive lifestyle. This includes maintaining sweet relationships and helping everyone with love, respect, acceptance, and a feeling of oneness, and to create an environment in which all relationships can grow and prosper. By criticizing others we assert our ego at the expense of others' feelings; and to criticize or believe false rumors, are mistakes that we make unknowingly, which will produce a dent in our positive thinking. Under such conditions, we need calmness, forgiveness, acceptance, and time, but not further interaction in the near future with these individuals. Giving time and waiting for a better day provides hope that in the future, when all are mentally and emotionally stable, the desired interaction will occur. When individuals do not believe in positive thinking and its need, we have to act with self-discipline, control, and utmost care, and continue motivating them, even if these attempts fail to produce positive thinking in others at that time.

To make our thinking positive, we require positive interaction with ourselves. Thus, we need to seek clarity in our thoughts, beliefs, actions, and decisions, and to perform all our responsibilities to the best of our abilities, without the expectation for recognition and appreciation from others. People should recognize our performance, and if they do not, we should be observant enough to realize these facts. Positive interaction without clarity and performance leads to positive thinking that is not true; and the same results occur when, having clarity, individuals believe in wrong principles and perform in the wrong way. These conditions indicate that clarity and performance should go hand in hand. Also, individual clarity and performance should contain global perspectives.

Keeping a positive state of mind requires a change in lifestyle that takes into account various factors, such as constructive thoughts, the understanding of others, motivation, selfless love, and prayer and worship. These factors are summarized in the formula: Positive Lifestyle = Positive Attitude + Positive Interaction with Self + Positive Interaction with Others. The mind can't be positive when the body is not; physical well-being and good health are prerequisites for peace of mind and positive energy.

8.1. Taking Care of Physical Health

Take time for everything. We have devised numerous means and machines to help us save time, but we make up new things that attack our time. It would be a rare person among us to hold forth on the virtues of virtue, and still rarer is the person who can walk his talk. It is very essential to maintain vitality and health so that our mind remains uncluttered because a cluttered mind destroys our peace and serenity. It is an acknowledged fact that people with low levels of vitality and energy are susceptible to all kinds of infections and diseases. So, practically speaking, the realization of a healthful body is mandatory to accomplish anything or have any chance in life. Although the necessary external tools or facilities may be available for a positive living, they are useful only if our mind, i.e., the internal machine, is ready. Thus, it is important to maintain our health under any circumstances.

There is a direct link between our physical health and the perspectives we hold. Norman Cousins hypothesized that individual beliefs and attitudes could either assist or complicate the process of healing. Our physical health is a reflection of our mental attitude. Some people are unable to overcome the negative programming of their parents, friends, or that of society. As a result, they become self-victimizing or self-sabotaging and beat themselves for everything that has gone wrong in their day. Therefore, it is essential that we know how to unduly relax and rest our body and mind. Our attitude for the day is extremely important. We should break the bad habits of thinking of our failures from the past or worrying about our future problems.

8.2. Incorporating Mindfulness and Meditation

The potential impact of the combination of physical activity and mindfulness/meditation cannot be overstated. For optimal health, regular moderate-to-vigorous physical activity is required to synergize with mindfulness. Together, they guard against loneliness and benefit every aspect of life, from reducing inflammation markers to improving decision-making. The well-documented anti-inflammatory effects of physical activity contribute to the health benefits of practicing mindfulness and meditation. Inflammation plays a role in everything from allergies to autoimmune disease. The relationship between exercise, mindfulness, and perceived stress also demonstrates why regular practitioners of both consistently enjoy better mental health. People tend to think of meditation as an exercise for the mind, but it is possible to focus on both the mental and physical aspects of well-being at once.

There is no denying the positive effects of mindfulness and meditation on the mind and the body. Mindfulness might very well be the cure for today's constant distractions. It allows our mind to free itself from stress and enjoy the precious present. Part of mindfulness is living in the moment, being aware of your surroundings, and truly immersing yourself in single-tasking. For researchers able to replicate the results with current advancements in functional neuroimaging, meditation, in particular, changes concerning negativity and the amygdala.

8.3. Engaging in Activities That Bring Joy

Seligman was also under no illusion about how stigmatized vigorous walking conversations were in academic settings. Despite feeling that those activities brought them the most joy, they doubted that these conversations were relevant to the research questions. Each knew that "together" and "conversation while walking" are impossible bedfellows. But as pioneering researchers, they took pride in asking the tough questions and demolishing paradigms. Because of this collaboratively competitive spirit, they continued to ask this question even though both believed it would not be central to the future of positive psychology. In a continuing display of optimism, they expressed, "Why not ask about the activity that brings the most joy?" The results summarize for all to see—a joyous surprise in a bitter field of hopelessness and depression.

Chris Peterson, Ph.D., raised a son with depression who died in his 20s. But Peterson was not a navel-gazing researcher, collecting data from the comfort of his lab. He was someone who faced tremendous adversity with optimism. Despite losing his son and the crippling suffering it brought, Peterson continued to be an intelligent, witty, and loving husband, parent, and mentor to the generations of young students he welcomed into his home. Bright children skateboarded on the wooden mantel above the fireplace. Unable to take himself too seriously, he would poke fun at his ballroom dancing, which he believed was the secret to his happy marriage.

CHAPTER 9

Spreading Positivity

The energy we generate in our interactions turns into a powerful force, but it's not hard to see that positivity may be more crucially important than any other sort of energy. Positivity affects how we perceive and interpret the world around us. It helps us to not only see opportunities but also recognize opportunities for what they can actually become. Being stuck in the doldrums affects our ability to take the real potential in the opportunities around us. When we look at the world this way, it's hard to deny the importance of positivity. By now, it should be clear that positivity is not only important for our psychological well-being but it's actually an essential part of our success in the world. Hedonism, optimism, and mutualism are tools that a leader can use to spread positivity throughout his or her sphere of influence: home, work, and society.

The energy and empathy we put into the world has a ripple effect, a force multiplier that we often overlook. In his book, Brian Tracy shares an example to illustrate this point. He explains that fire requires three components: heat, air, and a flammable object. If you remove any one of these, the fire will go out. Positivity is the same. It thrives in positive environments, and these positive environments we create become fertile ground for positive action and events. We are all vibrational beings. You have certainly heard someone described as having "good energy" or being "high vibration". Conversely, you have probably also heard someone described as being "negative" or "low vibration".

9.1. Being a Source of Inspiration

Positive-thinking people know they are role models, so they lead meaningful lives. Quantitative and qualitative evidence gives confidence in deploying strategies to gain a larger, or desired, positive mental attitude. A clinical doctor used her mental positiveness to help her breast cancer patients. Whatever the test results of an individual patient, she would anticipate success and full recovery for all. Her clinical and psychological practice paid off. Hospitals often refer serious cases for her to handle, knowing that her radical professional knowledge and loving care help sufferers of all diseases. Each time anonymously, patients' near-miraculous recovery leads to increased expectancies for a larger mental positivity.

Whatever state of mind you are in at any given time, it not only affects you in ways you do not consciously realize, some are subtle or even unseen. Today, high-tech electronic devices can detect human thought, and scientists can measure mental positiveness or negativeness in measurable quantities. So, to some extent, one person's negativity or positiveness can affect others. This is often the case when you hear someone viciously explaining why life is negative. That person's negativity can affect you if you allow it.

9.2. Encouraging Others

Be sure to encourage the people around you and help them grow their potential. Develop relationships that are beneficial for both of you by allowing them to discover their hidden beauty and strengths. Experience personal value and worth by recognizing and helping others increase their value and worth. Discover the path to happiness, significance, and meaning when you help the people around you realize who they are and what you believe in. When you encourage others to do and become their best, you help them become their highest and most powerful selves.

The more you encourage others, the more they will live up to their potential. Every person I talk to is looking for love and appreciation. The more I express compassion and appreciation to others, the better I feel. When you express appreciation for others, be sure to help them understand it is through their efforts, their will and perseverance that they have achieved what makes them special and unique.

9.3. Creating a Positive Impact in Your Community

It is particularly overpowering to see the various sources of untrue myths regarding the happiness of people who are wealthy. Contrary to what we are frequently told and what many people see, wealth doesn't buy happiness, excitement, or satisfaction. Assurance, success, and enjoyment may be decided by setting viable, significant objectives and working towards them bit by bit. And evidence has shown that spiritual individuals also have a greater sense of security and fellow kindness. There are significant projects that require your perseverance, vision, kindness, and help; undertake them with agony, tenaciously dealing with the obstacles that arise. There's no tolerance or magnanimity in expecting failure, so pursue your aims and perform the wonders your society has set aside for your entire life.

Once you have developed enough competence and security to develop yourself to the utmost, then you can begin to make a distinct contribution and start to get the elements of success in achieving your goals. This tangible connection to the community will aid you with the power of infinity and provide the style of motivation and commitment you require. Create an immense influence in society by being excellent and accomplishing your goals. You may possibly claim $500,000 in the lottery (which is rather less than a success to your targets and finding out eminence) and you can be very abundant, yet nobody is going to care. By achieving your aim, you are going to motivate others to begin to become the utmost model of themselves.

CHAPTER 10

Conclusion

We are all blessed to have a loving God who can turn each of us into something beautiful – if we let Him – if we trust. He works quietly and gently, rarely in big flashing gestures. Pray, acknowledge, and accept his gentle work in your life with gratitude and joy. Marvel at your progress and share your joy by doing good for others. Such is the recipe for reordering our lives. Honor His gentle love for you by saying, like St. Francis, "I am what I am before thee, O Lord, and nothing else." God will fashion you into a beautiful soul with a praiseworthy outlook. And as I often do, give thanks for His love that brings comfort and upholds you in the untouched child-like purity of your heart. Please, when you pray, remember Linda and Albert. They are a testimony to His touch in the Pearl of Great Price.

Each of us is a work in progress. We are all programmed with imperfections from the factory. Our challenge is not to let them dominate our outlook on life. Start with each negative thought, a positive wish. Take written notes on your progress. Very quickly, you will become aware of how often you engage in negative thinking. Knowledge is power; the power to change. Make these your ten commandments, and if you fail, start over and don't give up. Only you can make the changes that allow you to live the life and accomplish the things you were meant to. As Linda often says, "With God all things are possible, and without him, nothing is". God accepts and works with anyone who entreats him for his help.

Milton Keynes UK
Ingram Content Group UK Ltd.
UKHW031400011224
451790UK00009B/131